PIANO SOLO

DAVID LANZ – THE  LIFE

BIG SUR 2

KAL-E-FORNIA 10

THE GOOD LIFE 19

SORRY CHARLIE 27

MOOD SWING 35

MYSTICAL 40

IT'S THE WAY I FEEL 45

NOT A MOMENT TOO SOON 53

FOOL'S MAGIC 59

A SONG FOR HELEN 66

ISBN 0-634-08643-X

HAL•LEONARD®
CORPORATION
7777 W. BLUEMOUND RD. P.O. BOX 13819 MILWAUKEE, WI 53213

For all works contained herein:
Unauthorized copying, arranging, adapting, recording or public performance is an infringement of copyright.
Infringers are liable under the law.

Visit Hal Leonard Online at
www.halleonard.com

davidlanz.com

BIG SUR

By DAVID LANZ,
STEVEN DUBIN and JEFF LORBER

*All grace notes are played on the beat.

Copyright © 2004 by Moon Boy Music (BMI), Taste D Songs (ASCAP) and Songs Of Lorb (ASCAP)
All Rights Reserved   Used by Permission

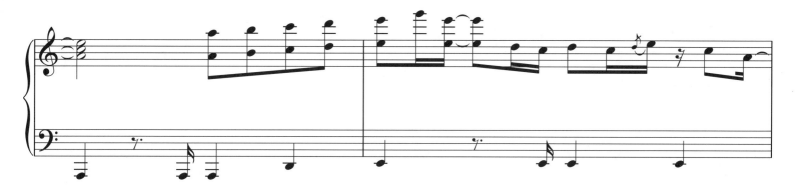

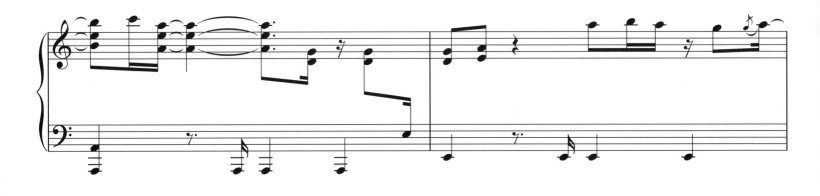

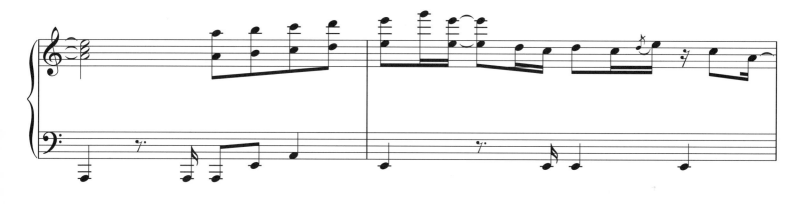

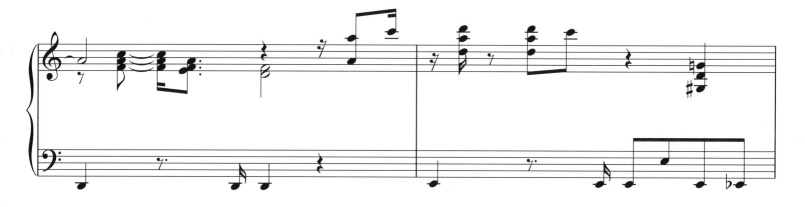

Sax (ad lib.):

Piano (ad lib.):

Sax:

Piano:

Sax:

Piano:

Repeat and Fade

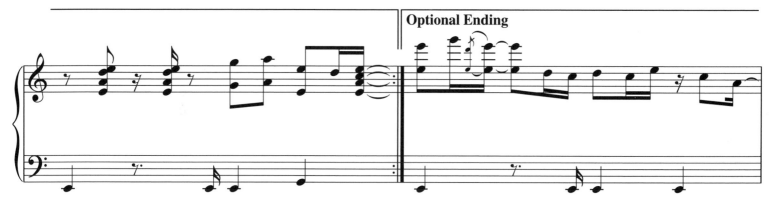

Optional Ending

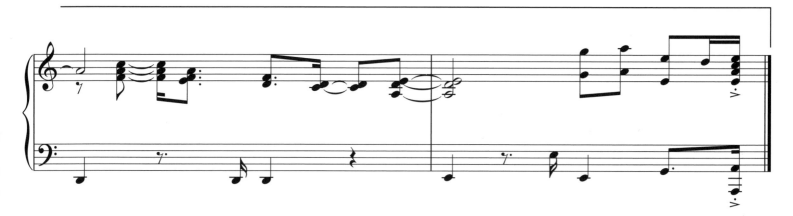

KAL-E-FORNIA

By DAVID LANZ

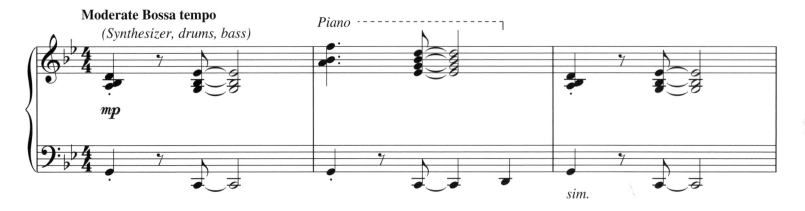

Copyright © 2004 by Moon Boy Music (BMI)
All Rights Reserved   Used by Permission

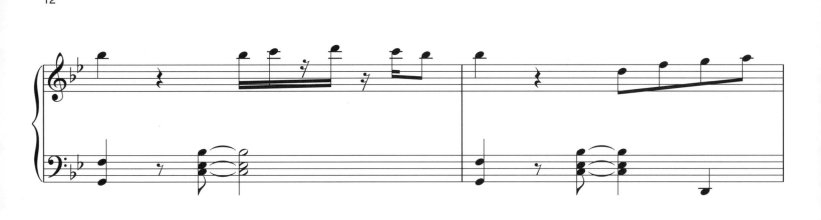

Synthesizer - - - - - - - - - - - - -

With pedal

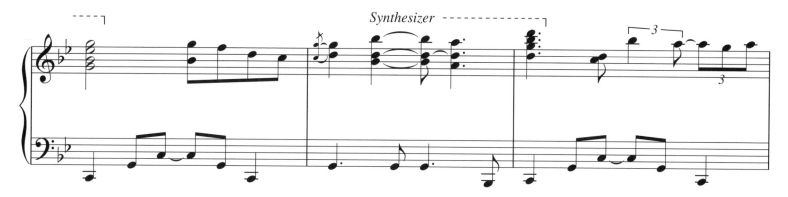

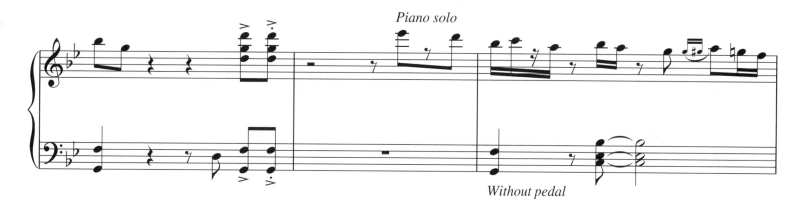

(Rhythm)

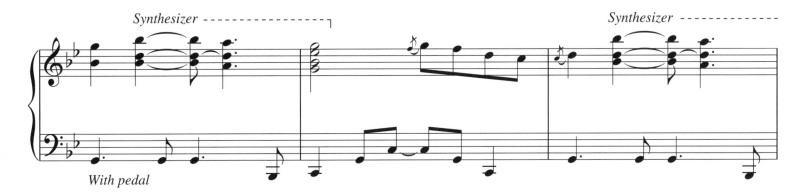

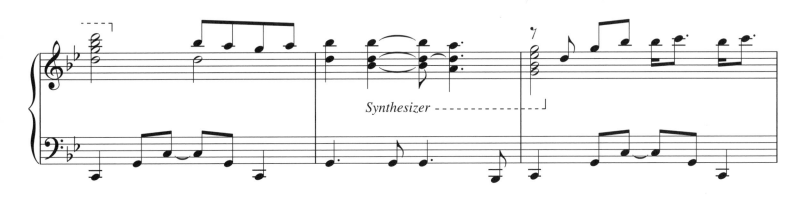

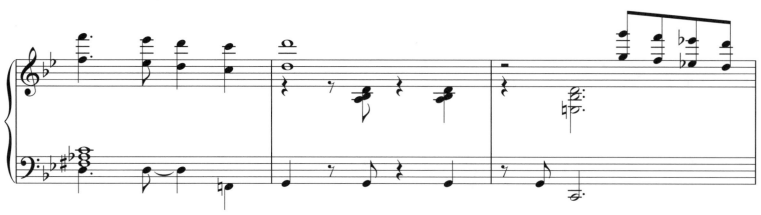

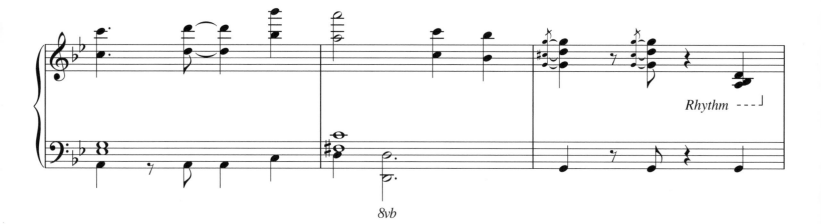

8vb

Rhythm ---⌐

Rhythm ---⌐

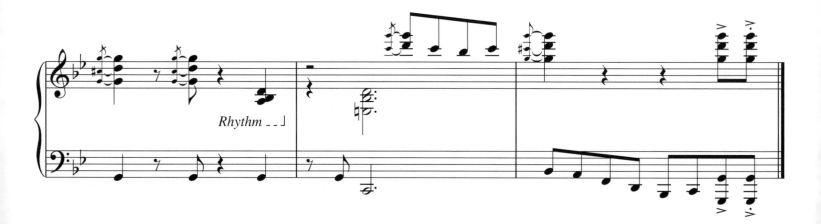

Rhythm ---⌐

THE GOOD LIFE

By DAVID LANZ

Sixteenth-note Shuffle

Guitar and Rhythm

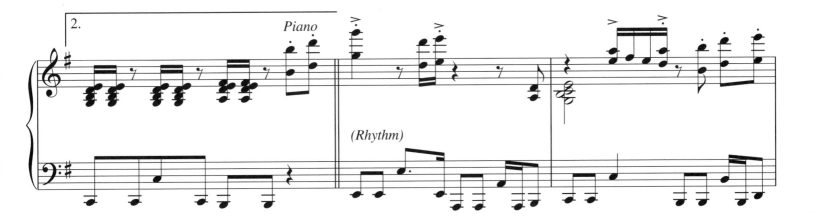

Copyright © 2004 by Moon Boy Music (BMI)
All Rights Reserved   Used by Permission

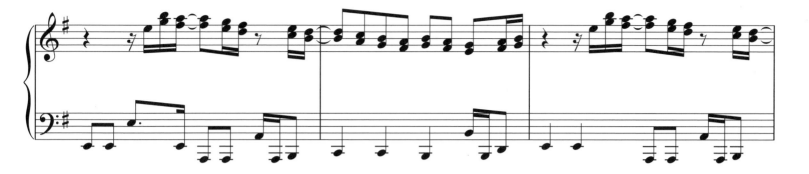

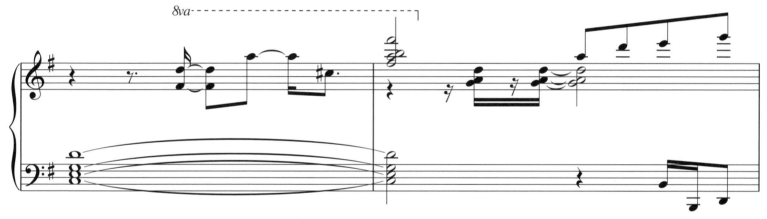

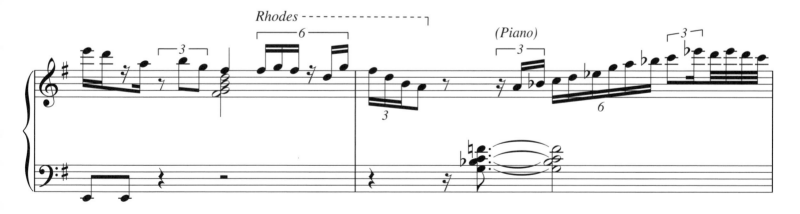

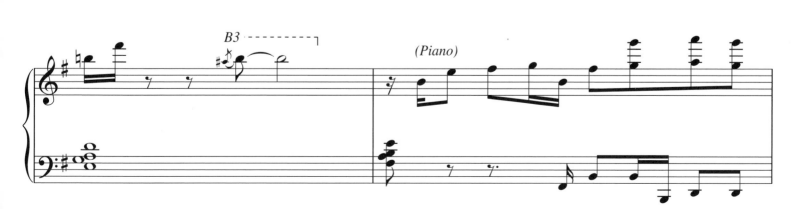

Begin fadeout...

SORRY CHARLIE

By DAVID LANZ

Copyright © 2004 by Moon Boy Music (BMI)
All Rights Reserved   Used by Permission

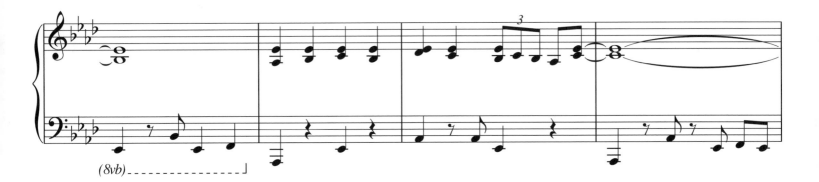

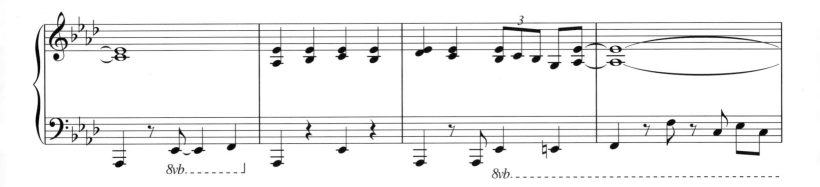

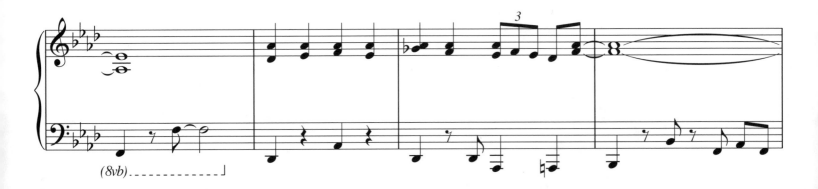

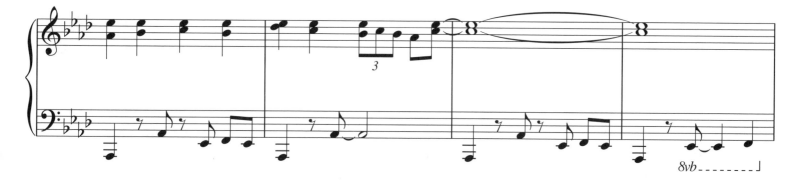

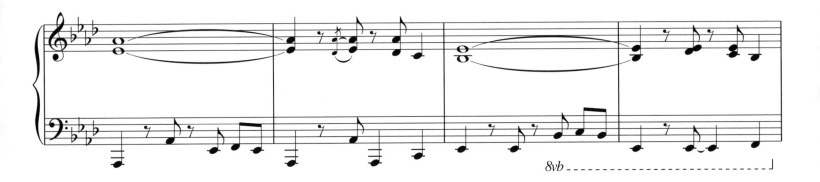

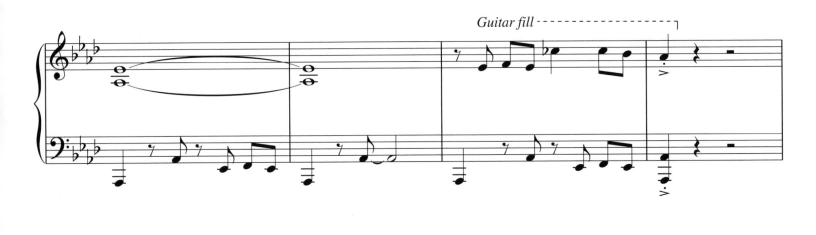

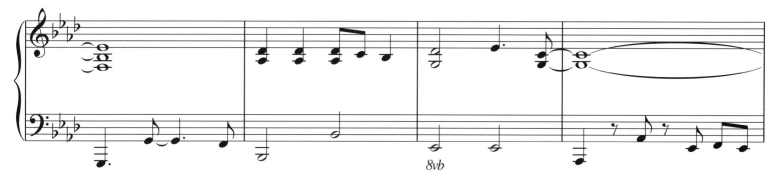

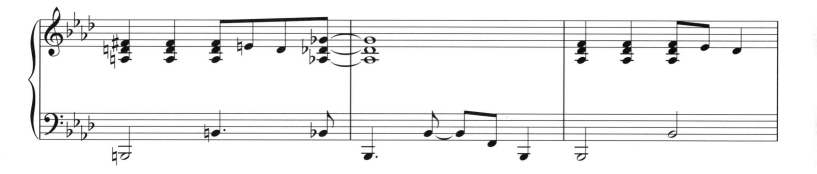

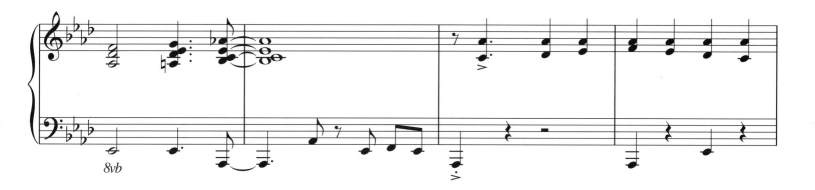

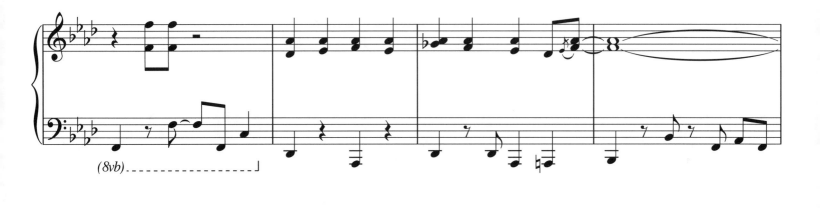

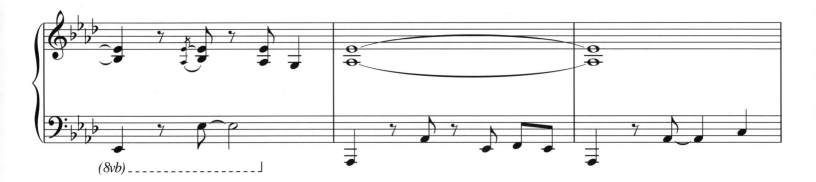

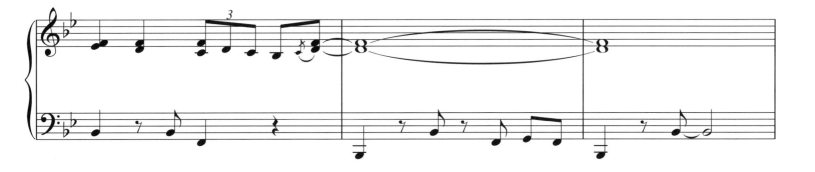

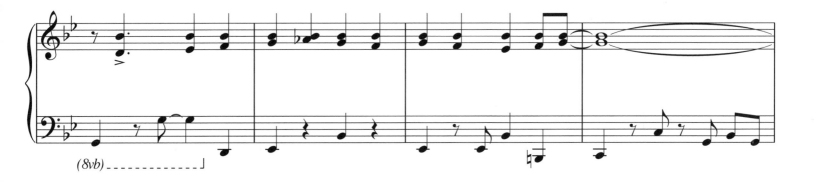

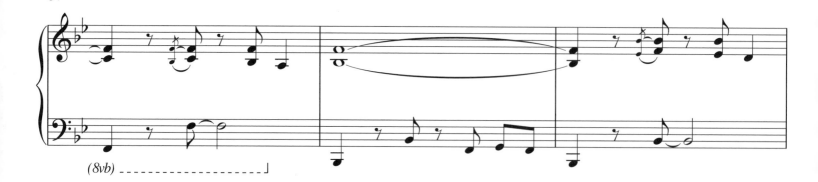

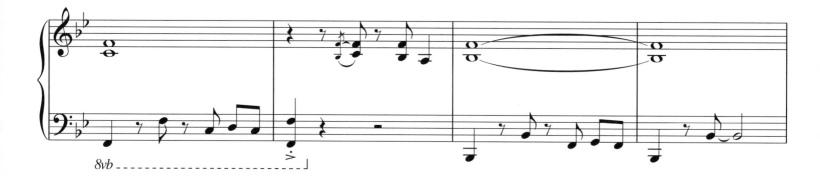

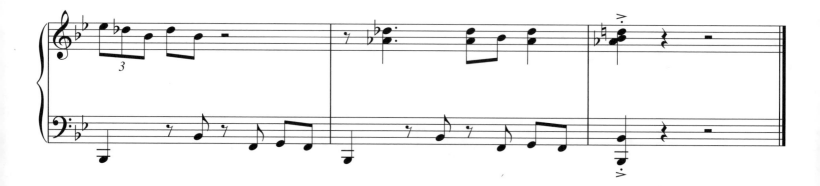

MOOD SWING

By DAVID LANZ, NELSON JACKSON,
STEVEN DUBIN and ROBBIE NEVIL

Funky

Copyright © 2004 by Moon Boy Music (BMI), Sony/ATV Tunes LLC (ASCAP), Ettafrancis Music, Inc. (ASCAP),
Ducfut Publishing (ASCAP), Taste D Songs (ASCAP) and R Nevil Music (ASCAP)
All Rights on behalf of Sony/ATV Tunes LLC, Ettafrancis Music, Inc. and Ducfut Publishing
Administered by Sony/ATV Music Publishing, 8 Music Square West, Nashville, TN 37203
All Rights Reserved   Used by Permission

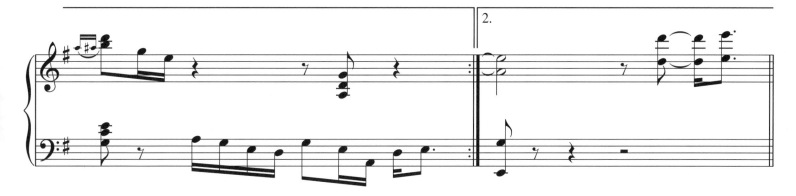

With pedal

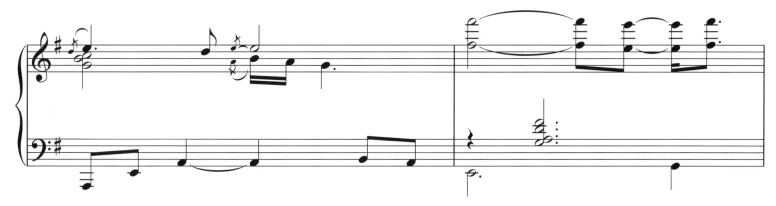

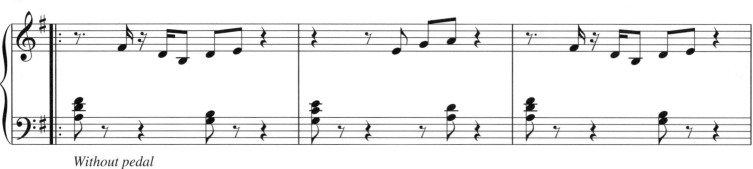

Without pedal

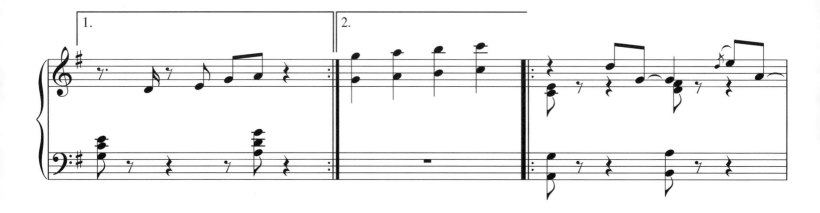

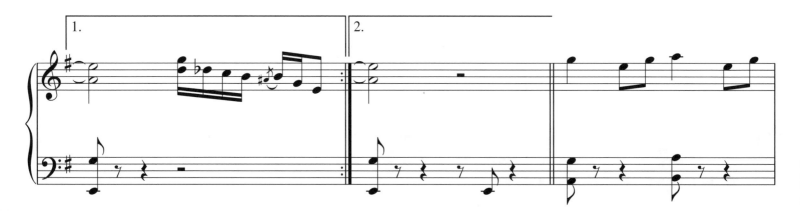

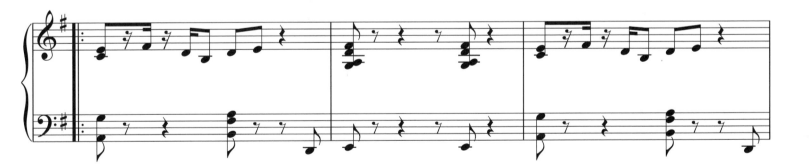

Repeat and Fade

Optional Ending

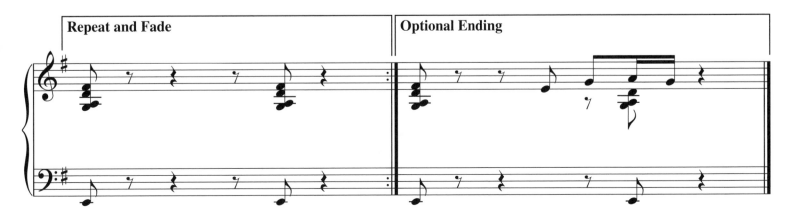

MYSTICAL

By DAVID LANZ,
STEVEN DUBIN and JEFF LORBER

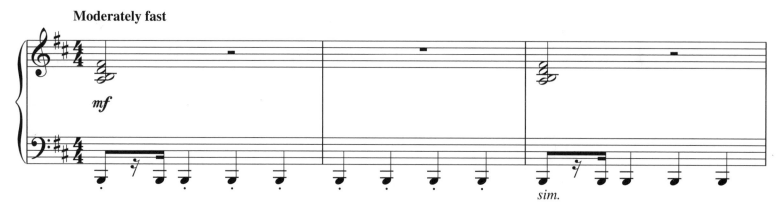

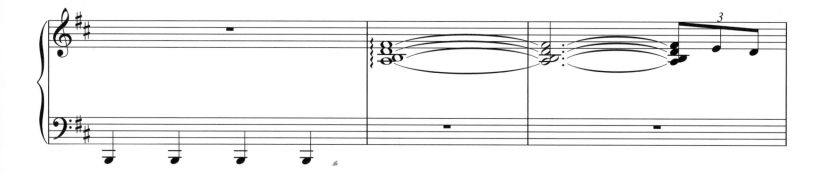

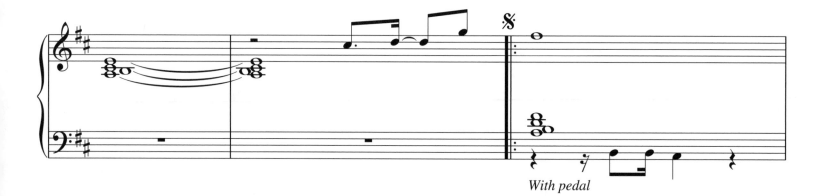

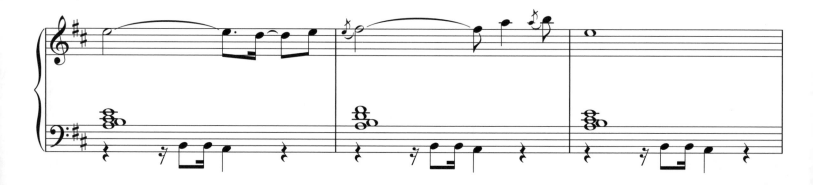

Copyright © 2004 by Moon Boy Music (BMI), Taste D Songs (ASCAP) and Songs Of Lorb (ASCAP)
All Rights Reserved   Used by Permission

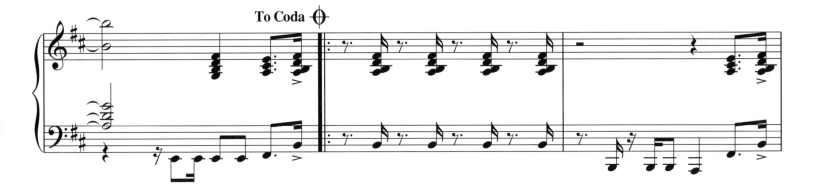

To Coda ⊕

1.   2.   D.S. al Coda
(take repeat)

CODA
⊕

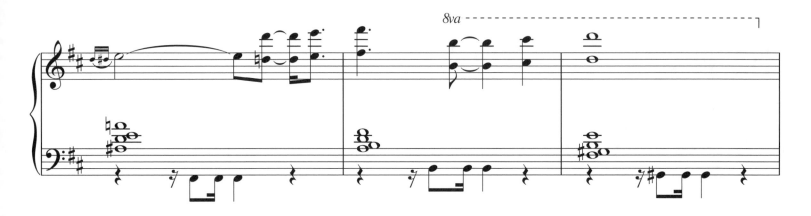

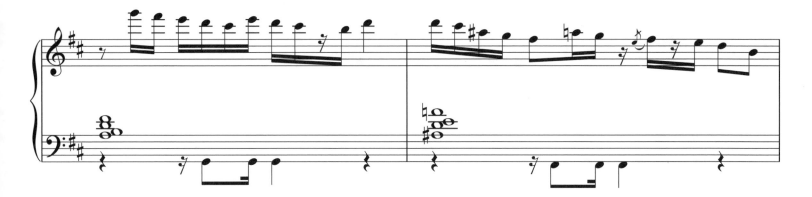

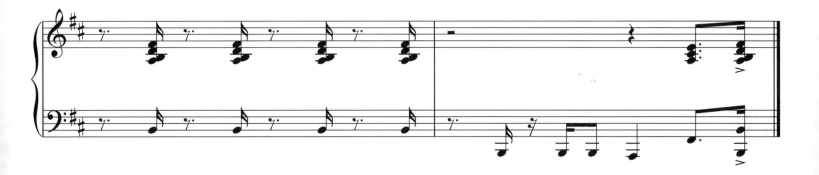

IT'S THE WAY THAT I FEEL

By DAVID LANZ

Moderate groove

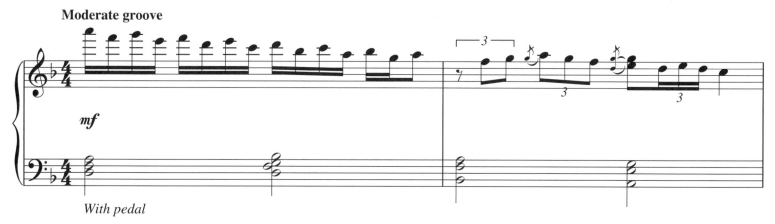

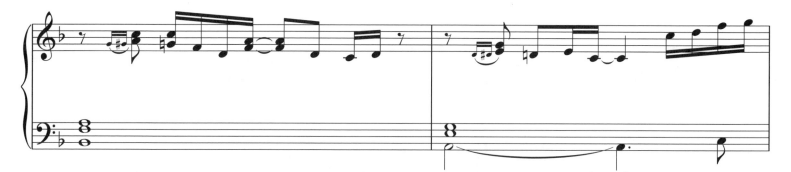

Copyright © 2004 by Moon Boy Music (BMI)
All Rights Reserved   Used by Permission

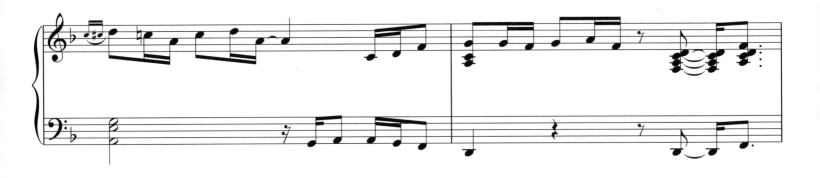

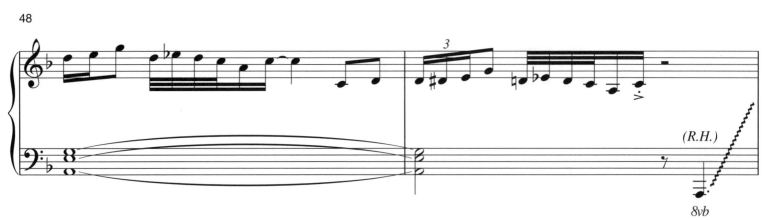

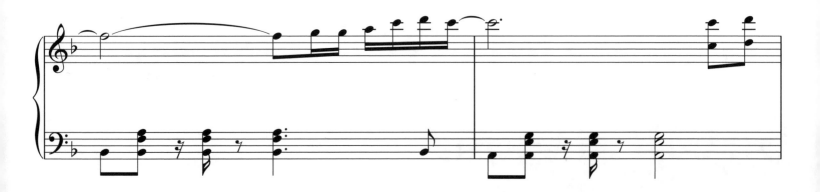

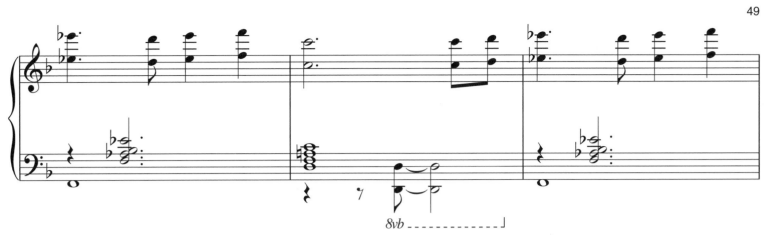

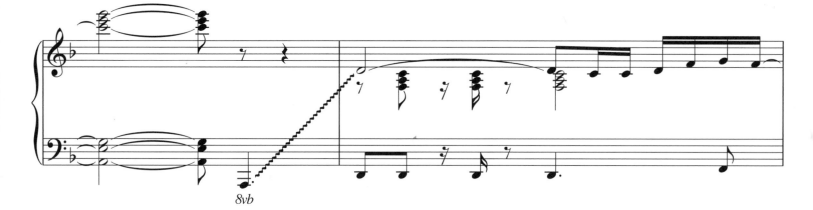

8vb

Piano solo:

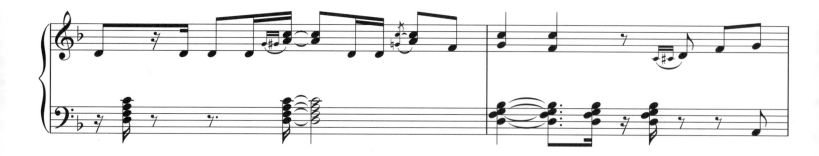

(Begin fadeout...)

Fadeout Ending

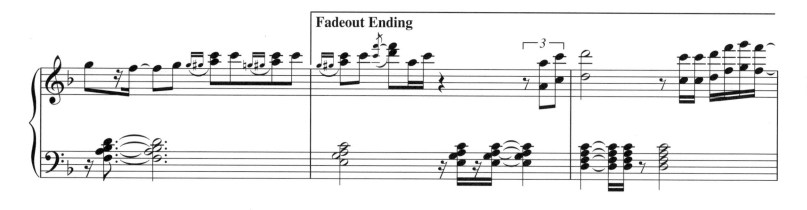

Optional Ending

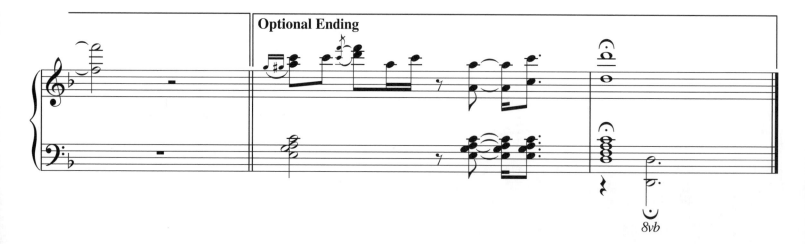

8vb

NOT A MOMENT TOO SOON

By NELSON JACKSON,
STEVEN DUBIN and ROBBIE NEVIL

Moderately

Copyright © 2004 Sony/ATV Tunes LLC, Ettafrancis Music, Inc., Ducfut Publishing, Taste D Songs and R Nevil Music
All Rights on behalf of Sony/ATV Tunes LLC, Ettafrancis Music, Inc. and Ducfut Publishing Administered by Sony/ATV Music Publishing, 8 Music Square West, Nashville, TN 37203
International Copyright Secured   All Rights Reserved

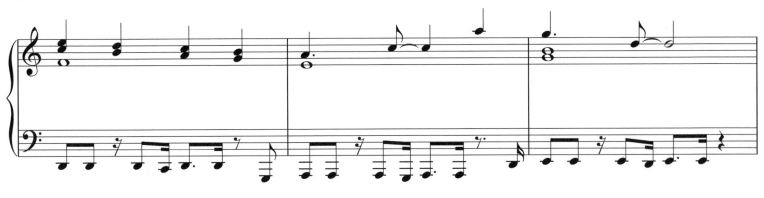

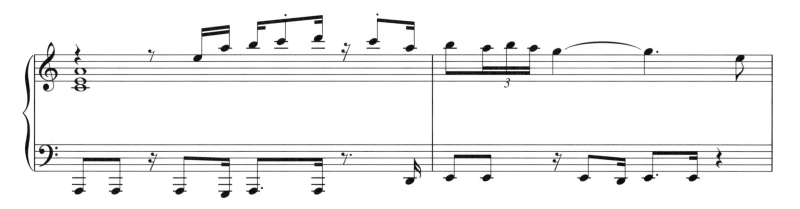

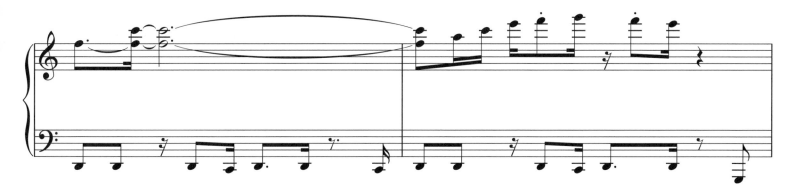

56

CODA

Sax solo:

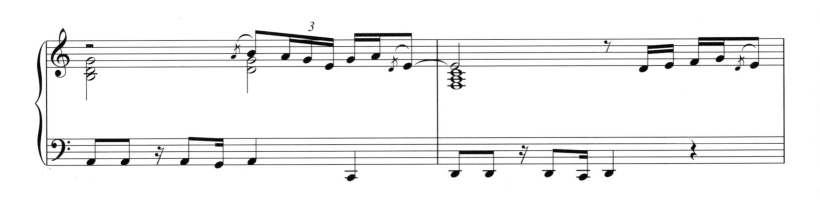

Piano:

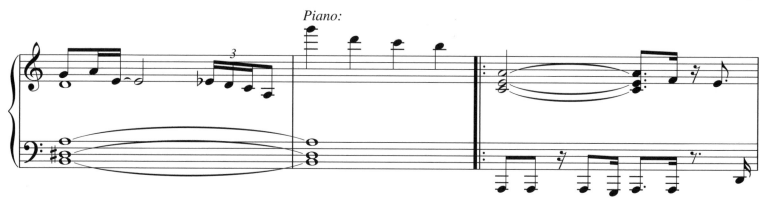

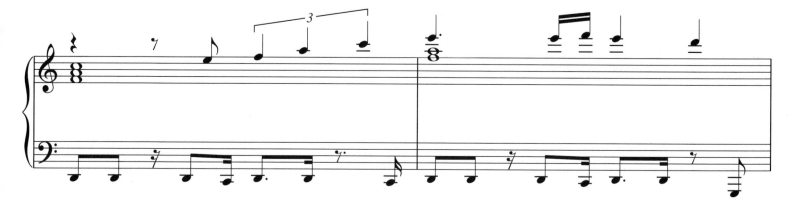

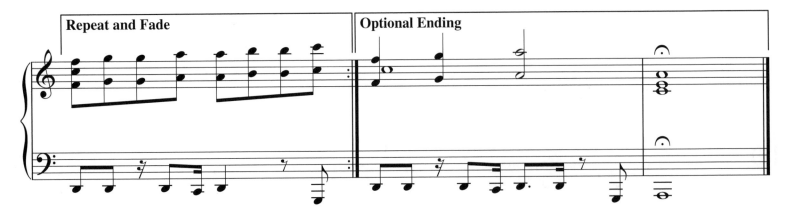

Repeat and Fade

Optional Ending

FOOL'S MAGIC

By DAVID LANZ

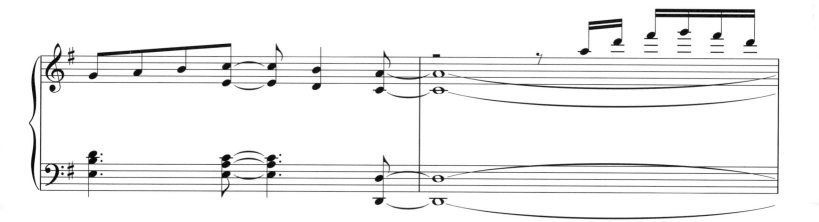

Copyright © 2004 by Moon Boy Music (BMI)
All Rights Reserved   Used by Permission

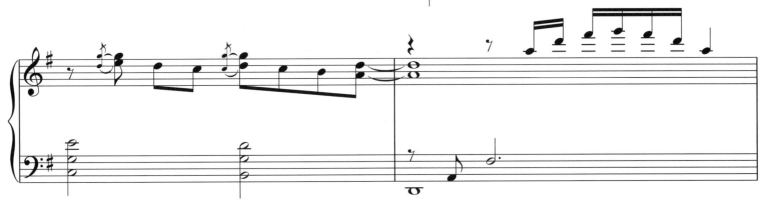

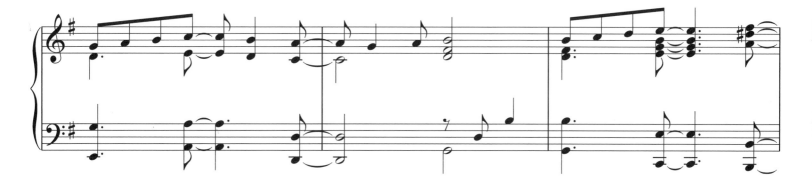

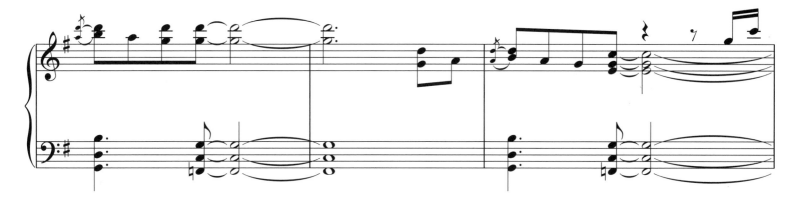

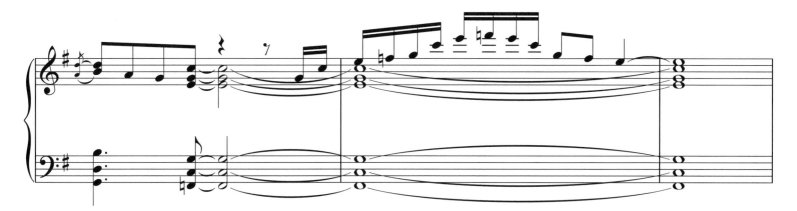

64

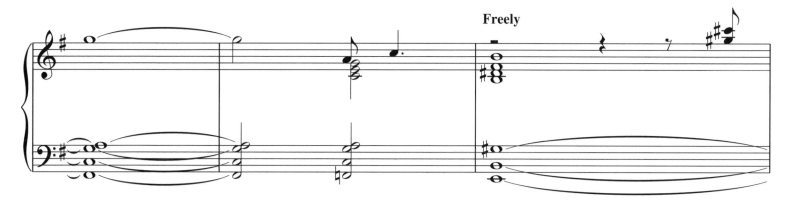

Freely

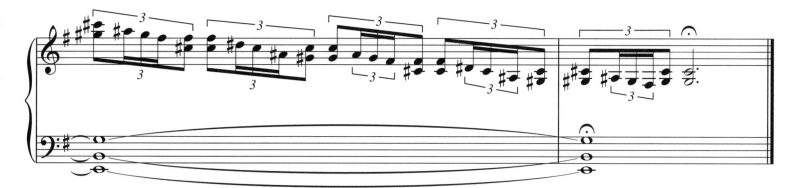

A SONG FOR HELEN

By DAVID LANZ

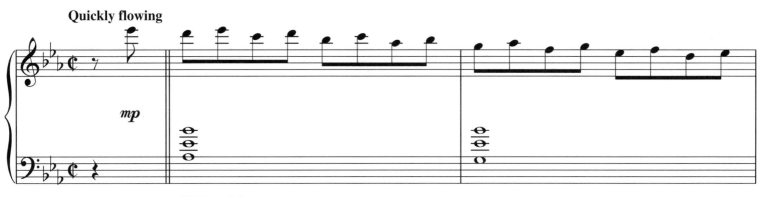

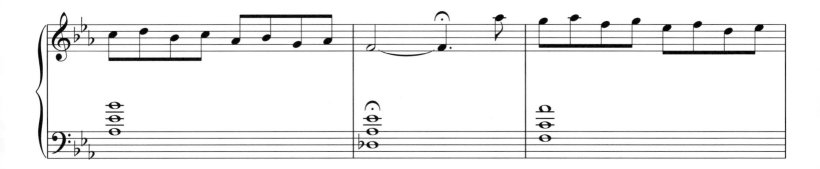

Copyright © 2004 by Moon Boy Music (BMI)
All Rights Reserved   Used by Permission

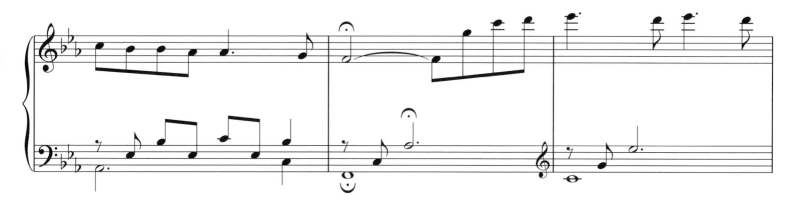

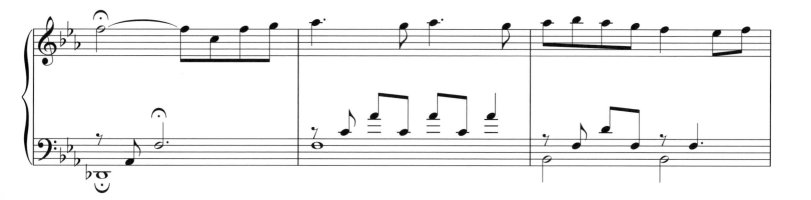

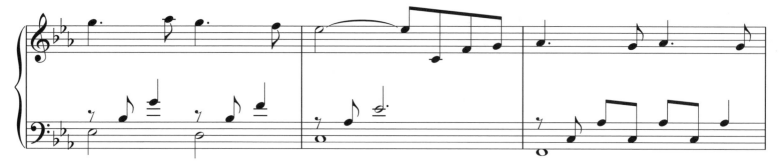

Expressively

70

Quickly flowing

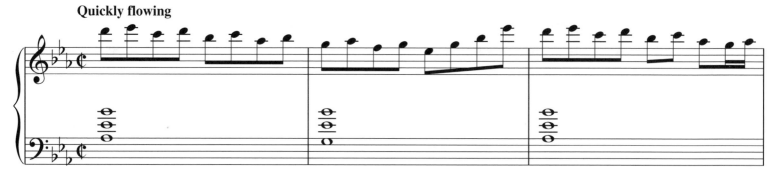

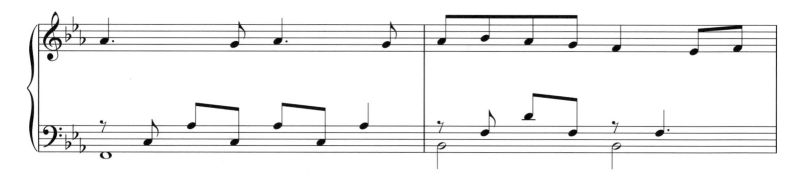

8vb

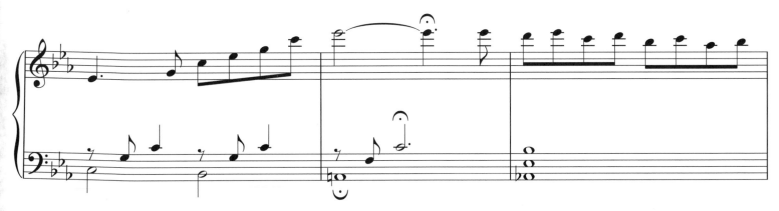